The Social Engineering Game Plan:

Information Gathering

Master the Art of Information Gathering & Target Selection.

Avoid Being Targeted.

DENNIS LONMO

The Social Engineering Game Plan:
Information Gathering

Copyright © 2018 by Dennis Lonmo. All Rights Reserved.

No part of this publication may be reproduced, distributed, or transmitted in any form or by any means, including photocopying, recording, or other electronic or mechanical methods, or by any information storage and retrieval system without the prior written permission of the publisher, except in the case of very brief quotations embodied in critical reviews and certain other noncommercial uses permitted by copyright law.

Dennis Lonmo

Visit my website at www.dennislonmo.com

Printed in the United States of America

First Printing: Sept 2018

ISBN: 9781723842061

Disclaimer

The goal of this book is to educate people about the techniques, approaches, and potential dangers involved in social engineering and to increase awareness of how people can better secure their information both on- and offline.

This book is not meant in any way to encourage people to use the knowledge imparted herein in pursuit of unethical or illegal activities.

Dennis Lonmo

What You Are About to Learn

Social engineering is no laughing matter. It can break both big organizations and individual human beings in a very short amount of time.

If you've ever been unlucky enough to be the target of a skilled social engineer, you probably don't know it. The number one skill of a social engineer is the ability to execute a successful attack without their target forming any suspicions whatsoever. Even the slightest suspicion from the target could potentially jeopardize everything. Think about it: When you start to become suspicious about somebody, even in a small way, that feeling tends to stick, right?

Most people know of social engineering as an integral part of hacking and the hacking culture. And yes, there are a lot of social engineers who spun out from hacking (or the other way around). But the best of the best, in either hacking or social engineering, tend to be really good at one of these fields, and not so good (even close to amateur-level) at the other.

It actually requires a very different skill set to do one versus the other. A traditional hacker is usually good with technology and numbers; a conventional social engineer, on the other hand, is generally good with people and psychology. If you find someone that's great at both, hire them, befriend them, or get to know them, because they are few to none.

In this book, we are going to talk about the human element of hacking, the aspect that we call social engineering. You're going to learn how a social engineer thinks; what resources they have; what kind of skill set they possess; and how they usually carry out attacks.

Now, why in the world should you listen to me? What can I teach you that you can't figure out by yourself and that may bring value to your life? My name is Dennis Lonmo, and I've been an entrepreneur since 2008. I've been involved in different industries and startups as well as my own business for the last decade. One thing, however, has stayed the same, and that is my consulting business. That business has and has ever had only one employee: me. And it was going to stay that way until I reach my final breath. My consulting business was the business I created myself, but it was not my first experience with the unique industry of social engineering.

As with most social engineers, my primary business has always been in some other field. You see, as soon as you parade around talking about how you're a great manipulator and social engineer, that you can trick anybody into telling you their secrets and revealing their classified information, you tend to lose friends and isolate yourself. Trust me, that's a fact. Nobody wants to have anything to do with a master manipulator on a regular basis. They only want you when they need you. That's what a lot of social engineering business models are built on.

In this book, you'll learn about information gathering—how social engineers gather information about their targets and what you can do to stop that from happening to you.

Acknowledgements

Thank you to everyone who made it possible for me to write this book.

To my fiancé. Thank you for taking care of our little girl and things at home while I disappear for hours and days to run my business and write these books. And also, thank you for trying your best to seem very interested in what I am doing, even though you have no clue what I'm talking about.

To my little princess. You are just about getting to that age where you start to miss me when I'm gone. I can tell you one thing: I miss you more than you can imagine, every time I walk out that door, morning and night, to go to the office. You're my cornerstone in life. You're not old enough to understand why I'm not there all the time yet, but someday, when you're older, I hope that you pick up some of my books and realize that everything I do in life is for you.

To my mom, who has always supported my professional endeavors, the way I live my life, and everything that comes along for me as a result. You're the most honest, straightforward-speaking person I know. Also to my step-dad, who despite major back issues and pain still came by every Monday, after finishing the day at your own job, to help me with my business all those years ago. You knew I had deadlines and was short-staffed, so you showed up without even being asked. I can't thank you enough for that.

Last but not least, to my friends. You're few but golden. Since we all have families and hectic lives of our own, we haven't gotten to hang out as much in recent years. But we do stay in touch, always. Even though we only see each other a few times a year, the jokes, laughter, the hard conversations, the advice, and the reality checks are priceless. Thank you.

Dennis

Contents Page

Chapter 1.
Introduction to Social Engineering

What is Social Engineering?

Social engineering is really nothing more than pure manipulation. You can add tools, technology, and any other factors to the mix, but, at the end of the day, everything comes down to an objective, a target, and a social engineer—in that order. Essentially, somebody has information that a company or individual is willing to pay a lot of money to get ahold of.

You could compare social engineering to spying. Have you ever seen the movie *Spy Games*? If not, you definitely should check it out. It has a lot of elements to it that actually aren't that far from the truth when it comes to the life and work of a social engineer.

To sum it up: A high-level social engineer will be an intelligent, manipulative, persuasive, and reflective individual with the ability to blend in anywhere.

Who is a Social Engineer?

A social engineer could be anyone, and anyone can become a social engineer. A lot of people don't think much about social engineers; they believe naively that they will never be victims of these attacks or that they will be able to smell trouble if they come anywhere near this kind of manipulative person. But it just doesn't make sense to have blind confidence in this matter—a skilled social engineer is not the person that everybody else in the room can see is a manipulative, evil individual. You could never make it as a social engineer if everybody you talked to became suspicious of you. It just wouldn't work.

In most cases that I've seen, social engineers are usually people with "normal" jobs and businesses. The vast majority of them have their own business because, in this line of work, they can't depend on a 9-5 situation. They have to be extremely flexible and available at all hours when they're working on a contract. They also tend to be the type to stick to themselves, as opposed to being party kings or attention-seekers. They're probably not the ones asking you to get drunk with them every Saturday night.

The very best social engineers are often "created" by their own past. How we have lived our lives since childhood has a pretty big tendency to determine the kind of natural skill set we develop as we mature. How we live our lives as young adults greatly impacts the person we end up becoming.

If you grow up in a life filled with lies and deceit, you end up trusting no one. You grow up feeling unloved and likely end up not being able to give love to others. You grow up as the black sheep, the scapegoat for everything wrong that happens to your family, and feel compelled to lie, fight, and manipulate in order to get what you want. In cases like this, the odds are you possess the skill set needed to make it as a social engineer. Now, there is no science to back up what I'm saying here—this is just a common background that the social engineers whom I know share.

The fact of the matter is that every one of the skills I listed above is crucial to a social engineer. Without these, there is no social engineer in the first place.

Skills to Expect

I've already mentioned some skills that you can expect a social engineer to show. But there is a whole range of talents and qualities a social engineer can possess. The ones above describe the broad and general skill set that a social engineer must have as a starting point, no matter what. But another vital skill to look out for is emotional control. A social engineer, more often than not, has a so-called "on/off switch" on their emotions, which means they can easily adapt to any situation to become or display what is expected of them in order to fit in. Whether it's a funeral or a birthday party, the social engineer has to be able to convincingly exhibit whatever emotions the situation calls for in order to gain the trust of the target(s).

This skill leads into the next: people skills. An engineer has to have a lot of insight into psychology—what makes people tick, what buttons to push to get the desired outcome, and more. Of course, as we are all individuals, we all react in our own unique way to different settings. That's where the engineer's level of psychological aptitude comes into play. Anybody can read about psychology and get familiar with how to push buttons and steer others in a desired direction; only a few, however, have the experience and knowledge to read not only the situation and emotions present, but also the individual human being.

This brings me to another skill: keeping emotions out of the equation. We are all humans, so we all have emotions that guide us through life, but some are more impacted by their emotions than others. A social engineer, however, has to keep every personal emotion out of the picture while on the job. If you easily get carried away with your emotions, not only could you not become a social engineer, but you would make for a great target in the eyes of one. A social engineer has to be cold and calculating to do what they do, or else they would lose their mind. Have you ever been nervous because you lied to someone to get something you wanted? Did you ever spill your guts to a friend and ended up a nervous wreck afterward because you were afraid that your secret would be outed? For a social engineer, conflicts like these are daily ordeals. Oftentimes a job could end up taking months or even years to complete. So, people who can't "leave work at work" in that kind of situation would be in the wrong business as a social engineer.

Another vital skill to have in this role is with technology. I have already briefly talked about the different skill sets between social engineers and hackers, but I want to clarify that a social engineer must have some degree of technical ability. At the very least, they must be able to use tracking devices, set up spycams, and plant ready-made malware (among other things). But the engineer should also be able to use tools like Maltego and SET (Social Engineering Toolkit), which are programs which can be utilized to find information about an individual and to launch phishing attacks, among other things. We'll get to more on this subject later on in the book.

Social Engineer Shapes and Sizes

I've now covered what and who a social engineer could potentially be. There are, however, different kinds of social engineers. Not all of them call themselves social engineers, but more often than not, they all share the same objective. They just have different approaches in achieving it.

The first one I would like to mention is the individual engineer. This type of social engineer usually works alone, with no partner, aide, or backup. The reasons many prefer this method is: 1) There is less chance of anything going south. Nobody is around to fuck up or blow the whistle on you. 2) The ability to pick and choose. You only have yourself to worry about, which means you can choose the jobs you want and say no to the rest. You don't have to worry about putting food on anyone's table but your own. 3) More complex jobs. Believe it or not, working alone often increases your ability to take on specific tasks which with a team would be infeasible. The reason for this is that you can maximize your skill set on your own; you don't have to train employees to master some skill that they don't naturally possess. You can always work on your own best skills. 4) Money. With more complex and long-lasting gigs come higher paychecks.

The second type worth mentioning is the team. A team is usually composed of talented individuals that together cover all aspects of the hacking umbrella. Some of them are expert hackers; others are experts in entering buildings and bypassing security systems; others are strategists; and still others are basic social engineers. A team can take on bigger, more comprehensive, and varied jobs on their own without having to outsource or make use of contractors. However, there are more people involved in a project from start to finish, which means a possible decrease in the mission success rate in this sort of business. There are a lot of moving parts and a lot of individuals who have to perform at peak level throughout the job; so, to manage these and to also achieve results every time calls for an exceptional group of individuals. Some businesses manage to do this to perfection.

There are a lot of different types of social engineers, but these two are the most common. Another honorable mention would be the type who is employed by businesses in various unrelated industries, lumped together with those who use their primary (social engineering) skills as a hired gun in those various industries. For lack of a better word, you might call this type "white label social engineering."

The Weakest Link

As human beings, we are flawed in every sense of the word. Isn't it surprising that even with that knowledge, businesses and corporations still prioritize securing their technology, to the extent that their human resources are neglected? Big chunks of the typical security budget are being poured into firewalls, detections systems, and tech personnel. But as for the human element? Management, employees, and staff are lucky if they get to go and hear somebody speak about security protocol once every couple of years.

The issue that gets lost in this dilemma is this: If somebody wants information from a business on a particular topic, they would typically much rather "go and get it" themselves than spend weeks or months pounding away at a system that they may not ever gain access to in the end. Humans, however, have needs; they have emotions; they feel; they're greedy and hungry for power, no matter how delusional it may be; and they inevitably make mistakes, every day and all the time. It's just human nature. And human nature is very much exploitable.

Why Does Social Engineering Exist?

Social engineering is widely used by corporations, governments, criminal enterprises, and even medium to small businesses worldwide. With the rapid changes in the economy and technology and massively increased global competition, social engineering is used for national, industrial, criminal, and competitive intelligence.

As with traditional hackers, we have three main categories for social engineering: white hat, grey hat, and black hat.

White Hat

This kind of engineer follows the rules and regulations of the country in which the job is performed to the teeth. He will not break or even bend any laws in order to get the information he's after. The primary sources of information for these kinds of engineers are what is readily available on the web. Sources may be news sites, company sites, and public records. White hat social engineers work only for legitimate businesses and corporations.

Grey Hat

This is the category where you'll find the engineers who use information and tools which are not always publicly available. The way grey hat hackers work can in most cases be considered ethical and legal. They may bend, twist, and in some cases break the rules, but we are not talking about serious crimes or people getting hurt; we're talking about rules that are similar in theory to speeding or parking tickets. The fact that these engineers are willing to go an extra length and do these kinds of things without anybody being hurt and are still able to produce results makes them highly attractive to potential employers. Grey hat social engineers mainly work for legitimate businesses, but some could be considered "mercenaries" by virtue of the fact that they follow the money—even if it leads them to work for potentially criminal organizations.

Black Hat

These are the people who will do what it takes to complete the task they're given without any regard toward rules, laws, and others' well-being. You won't find these guys with a simple Google search; they're on the other side of the table than the other types of engineers. It's easy to draw parallels to simple con men (the "snake oil salesmen") when we talk about black hat social engineers. The problem is that some of them—not even close to the majority, but some—have really dangerous skills.

Grey hat engineers will often get the results that they're after, but the chief difference between that type and black hat is that the former actively prevents victims from noticing that anything is happening and allows them to go on living life as they were before. The black hat, on the other hand, usually don't care what happens to their victims, nor the state of their feelings, either during the process or after exploitation.

Chapter 2.
Technical Information Gathering

At this point you know a lot about social engineers, what they are, who they are, and why this industry exists. The next step is to learn some tactics they use to gather information.

The first thing any social engineer does when starting an assignment is gather information. What's important to know when doing information gathering is that there is *a lot* of irrelevant and useless information out there. They have to be able to navigate through all the bullshit to find the information that matters. The internet is vast, and there is a sea of information out there on individuals like you and me. If the engineer were to try and fetch it all, finding the right target and eventually building a profile would be almost impossible, considering the time needed and all the useless and incorrect information that would be used to get to the next step. Therefore, social engineers must know what to look for, where to look for it, and how to compile all that valuable information into target profiles.

Dradis

Before starting to gather information, it could come in handy to use a tool to store all the collected information in one place.

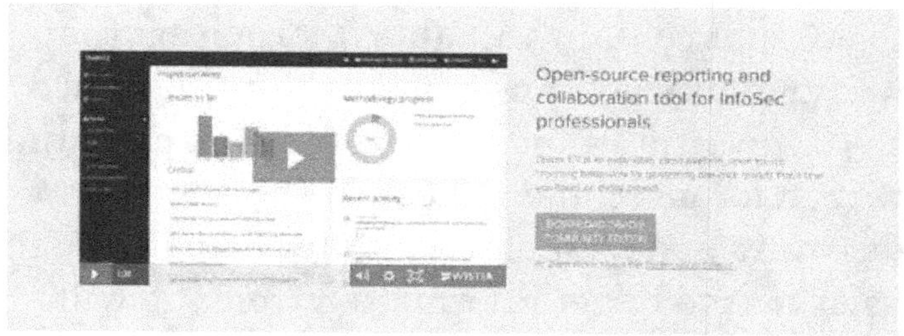

Dradis is one such tool. Dradis is really a web application that provides a centralized repository that helps you organize, keep track of, and share information. It's a popular choice for security specialists worldwide. It has extensions that allow you to integrate with a lot of hacking tools, such as Metasploit, Burp Suite, NMAP, and more. Moreover, it has a community edition that's entirely free for use. You can check it out here: https://dradisframework.com/integrations/.

Blogs

Disgruntled employees, management, and even contractors tend not to be very confident about their information if they've fallen out of favor with their employer, business partner, or others. There are numerous blogs on the web today that contain valuable information that would in any other circumstance be classified as confidential—and these could be a potential way in for a social engineer. If the engineer discovers an ex-employee of the company he's been tasked to get information from, he will scour the web for information about and from that individual. If that individual has a hatch to grind with the employer and has been careless with his information by posting something in pure anger on his personal blog, for example, that would present an excellent opportunity for the engineer to make contact with him. The engineer would reflect the same resentment that the ex-employee feels in his communication and build a relationship from there in order to get more information from him.

Social Media Recon

Every social engineer on the planet won the lottery a few years back. The introduction and explosion of social media made their job a heck of a lot easier. All that information gathered in one place, just waiting to be plucked.

The carelessness that comes with these platforms, compounded with the desire to display everything one possesses—money, cars, house, pets, family—actually creates an illusion of safety for the users. Because *everybody does it.* Everybody is sharing these things with the world nowadays. But this custom couldn't be further from "safe."

If you're the kind of person that displays everything on social media, don't care about privacy, and put stock in the number of friends you have or the number of likes you get on a post, you make for an excellent target for a social engineer.

Everything an engineer needs to know could potentially be collected from an individual's social media account. Think about it for a second: Not so long ago, information like birthdates, family, interests, close friends, vacations, money, and jobs was something that wasn't publicly advertised.

To get that information the social engineer had to do a lot of work—talk to people, get close to individuals close to the target, perform some old-fashioned recon, and put in a ton of hours, but that's not necessary anymore. Because of the rise of social media.

Maltego

No matter how much information the social engineer has collected, there is a tool that everybody in their field loves to use. It is called Maltego.

With Maltego, engineers can gather information about anybody, as long as that information exists somewhere on the web. It grabs data from DNS records, APIs, social networks, search engines, and more.

What makes Maltego even more valuable is that it not only collects the information, but it then displays it in a useful way. Let's say the target has a lot of information about themselves on different websites.

Maltego would be able to analyze the relationship between all that data from the various websites and return something like, "target's email address found on six learning platforms."

Using Maltego the right way helps a social engineer build a profile and set up a viable plan to execute their task. We'll talk more about Maltego and how it is used later on.

Telephone Call

Making a simple telephone call could potentially yield real nuggets of information that the social engineer would have a hard time getting their hands on by any other method. But the golden age of phone calls is over.

An engineer can't really rely on using this technique on anybody anymore, as we have switched from calling to texting; from talking for hours on end, to barely having the time to take the call.

The most damaging evolution of telephoning (from the social engineer's standpoint) is that of phone sales. The degree which this issue has been negatively covered in the media in the last decade has made a lot of us suspicious even before we pick up a call. Just hearing the phone ring has us on edge (because it might be a salesperson trying to sell us something or a con man trying to talk us into giving him our money).

This doesn't apply to everybody—that goes without saying—but the shift in how we view phone calls has been happening for a long time.

Phone call cons are most commonly used by social engineers on the wrong side of the law with more general and broad-ranging objectives, like credit card schemes.

The targets are usually elderly people who more likely don't have an in-depth knowledge of technology yet or haven't adapted to the modern mindset. They may have grown up in a past time where respect and honor was the way of life, and may wish to preserve that attitude in the world that we live in today; but unfortunately this makes them easy targets for scam artists and black hat social engineers.

The telephone is still used in attacks today for the purposes of gaining access or trust, pretending to be someone else, fake surveys, and similar cons. We'll get more in depth about that in another book of this series.

Chapter 3. Information Gold Mines

Websites

Every company has a website nowadays. Modern marketing techniques such as building trust with costumers, transparency, and appearing authentic to potential clients without ever meeting them, all has to be done through websites. What this means for social engineers is that a lot of valuable information about a company and its employees can be found on their website. By manually crawling a site, the engineer can collect information such as locations, employee names, phone numbers, email addresses, images, bios, and usually a ton of valuable information about the people in the top management positions.

Remember what I said about transparency and authenticity being so important between businesses and their clients nowadays? Well, that priority almost guarantees the information collected on these sites to be correct.

Search Engines

Everybody uses a search engine, right? When you want to find something, you just search for it and check out the results the search engine returns to you. That's a process *everybody* is aware of—so why am I discussing it in the chapter on "Information Gold Mines"?

Well, earlier in the book I briefly talked about social engineers' ability to find relevant information without spending time on useless gathering which in the end doesn't yield any useful results. For their purposes, common search queries are out of the question, as they just won't suffice in getting the desired returns. To get relevant results, social engineers use queries like this one: *inurl:"Name"*.

This query will return every page on the web that contains "name" in the URL. Another example is to use the query *"Name"intitle:"email""phone"*. A query like this will return everything about *"Name"* that has titles with information like email address and phone number.

So, there are numerous ways to get information you need on regular old search engines. You just have to know where and what to look for.

Pipl

This website is in many ways THE gold mine for social engineers. Pipl stores all the information it can collect on an individual in one place; it's free to use for everybody; and it prides itself on being the world's largest people search engine.

The service Pipl offers is not illegal—heck, it even provides solutions to some of the biggest companies out there, like Twitter, Microsoft, and eBay.

If you take a moment and think about what you just learned, you're probably going to end up with the conclusion that there really is no such thing as privacy on the web.

Maybe reading this book is a wakeup call for you, and maybe you'll start to think twice before posting a particular piece of information about yourself on the web.

Whois.net

Thought it is considered by many to be a place where you search for domains to see whether they are available for purchase, Whois.net is so much more than that.

If a social engineer wants to get their hands on some information about a target's domain name, the only thing that needs to be done is a search on that domain on a website like Whois.net. Whois.net is kind of a search engine in itself; you search for a domain, and it returns all the information it can get on that particular domain: information such as the domain registrar, IP address, name servers, the name of the owner, address of the owner, and more. It is not as much of a gold mine as

Pipl potentially is, but depending on the information the social engineer needs, it can be precisely the right tool to use.

Chapter 4.
Physical Methods

A lot of times, technical methods just won't be enough to create an accurate profile of a target. After all, the goal may be a tech-savvy individual who knows a thing or two herself about hacking and social engineering. Heck, maybe she even read this book. In most cases, good old physical engineering is required to achieve a complete profile.

When working a social engineering job, the engineer will after a while feel the need to connect with the target somehow. Not in the sense of hanging out and becoming friends with them (we'll get to that later in this series); but rather, to see them up close and in person. To know what they are doing and when they are doing it throughout the week. This is information that's hard to attain just by sitting in front of a computer, and it is knowledge that is invaluable when the engineer is preparing the next phase of their attack. That's why physical information gathering still does, and more than likely will continue to, play a huge role in social engineering.

Dumpster Diving (One Man's Trash Is Another Man's Treasure)

Yes, literally. Going through a company's trash can prove to be a very profitable endeavor. "Dumpster diving" covers everything from digging through outdoor containers to turning a little trash can upside down to see what falls out. And believe me, you would be surprised to see what kind of sensitive information gets thrown away. Times are changing; you might think that the social engineer would have a hard time getting confidential information from trash cans now that there is less paper and more digital communication. Well, that's not the case. Paper shredders have existed "forever" in one form or another, but a lot of businesses are very sloppy with mandating and enforcing what goes into the shredder versus the paper trash can.

The reality of less paper being used than ever before, however, has impacted how paper documents are handled. Companies spend money on tech security, that's a fact. But I've been relatively surprised over the last few years about the lack of security around papers; since things are largely turning digital, companies don't even seem to think that printed documents present any threat at all anymore. And that's a big mistake. You see a lot of people choosing to print a document unnecessarily—even though they might receive it as a PDF file ready to sign and send digitally—just to view it and later sign it digitally anyway. What happens to that printed document? It often ends up right in the trashcan, without ever visiting a shredder.

Some of the documents a social engineer would be on the lookout for when dumpster diving are business cards of employees, suppliers, and contractors, contracts, proposals, ID cards, used smartphones, and other documents and tech equipment. A dumpster reveals some interesting facts about its owner—it's not just a way to get your hands on documents or equipment. It also tells you a lot about the company's routines or lack thereof, which further shows you whether they prioritize security. Information like that is in itself an excellent indicator of what kind of "resistance" a social engineer will be met with when trying to complete their objective.

Surveillance

Familiarity with the comings and goings of a target throughout the day will help a social engineer better understand their day-to-day life. You've probably seen stakeouts portrayed in movies, and this is much of the same thing. A social engineer has to physically have eyes on the target for a certain amount of time to learn more about them. When do they wake up and go to work? Where do their family and neighbors work and what are their schedules? Does the company have 24/7 surveillance, do they use ID cards, access cards, security systems, physical security, or other security measures and are they in place around the clock? Does the target engage in suspicious behavior or associate with known criminals, and does this give the social engineer any leverage?

All of these questions need to be answered in order to proceed with the objective. If the engineer finds something unique, like questionable behavior or associates, it opens the door for potential leverage that the social engineer can stealthily implement into the attack.

Piggybacking

Once the social engineer has learned a bit more about the target's routines, it becomes time for piggybacking.

Piggybacking refers to the art of gaining access to otherwise secure areas by piggybacking off somebody else who already has access to those areas—usually employees or contractors of the target business. People don't want to be known as paranoid, so they'll generally do everything in their power to stop people from forming that impression of them. We also like to be helpful whenever we can. These two personality traits are a social engineer's most significant advantages when it comes to piggybacking.

Let's say you work at a place where the doors to the offices automatically lock whenever they close. You, being afraid to be perceived as paranoid, usually walk in the door without ever looking behind you or otherwise making sure the door locks itself after you pass through. The social engineer could just walk in straight behind you, or maybe place something over the locks so that they won't function when the door closes, and come back later, at a less obvious time.

Or, let's say the building you work in has physical security that checks your ID whenever you enter the building. The social engineer could dress up in the exact same way the employees at the business typically do, wait for you to enter, and then try to get past security. This will only work in some cases; the key to success is the social engineer's ability to act in the same manner that the employees usually do. Know the first and last name of at least one of the security guards and make a move a couple of minutes after the employees should have clocked in so that they appear to be a justified hurry. The punchline in this scenario is that the engineer has forgotten their ID card at home, which is "understandable" to the security guard, as they are clearly running late to a meeting or to work. The social engineer is taking advantages of multiple factors that are at play every day in any human being: the will to help others; the sense of respect and confidence humans get when someone they have never met calls them by their full name; and the logic of this very normal, unsuspicious situation. Nothing throws the security guard off. Every aspect of the social engineer's con only enhances the

security guard's conclusion that this person
really does have an appointment inside the
building and needs to get there in a hurry
because other people—like the security
guard's boss—is waiting for this individual
right now. Does the guard give the social
engineer access? Generally, this plan works
incredibly well for the engineer. It is a
prevalent method for entering offices in order
to gain a first glance at what's inside.

Entry

When the engineer gets access to a house, building, or office, the next phase of the information gathering process begins. You might think that they take a look around to get an overview of the facilities and then get the hell out. But no, that's usually not the case. Whenever access is granted to a place that has the potential of revealing confidential information concerning a target or even the final objective, the engineer starts to work on how to attain that information without raising any suspicions. The ways to do that is by old-fashioned "bugging" (planting microphones), taking subtle photos (always having a camera on the body), and planting cameras if applicable. While doing this, there is also a need to look out for additional security measures and to try to locate the sensitive areas inside the offices without raising any eyebrows. If the objective is inside the building, then the building is itself the target. In these cases, the social engineer must try to achieve as much as possible in a short amount of time. If there are any documents lying around—any at all—they must be secured. There's no time to read then and there; the objective is just to obtain as much information as needed and then to get out of there in style, so that nobody thinks twice about why the engineer was there in the first place.

Chapter 5.
Targeting

One or Several

When a certain amount of information surrounding the objective is gathered, the social engineer has to narrow down their list of potential targets (or ways in). As tempting as it can be to have multiple targets, the engineer should be left with one, and only one, main target at the end. You might think, why? Throwing more balloons up in the air increases the chances of one landing on your head in the end, right?

True, but not helpful in this case. Social engineers' primary objective is to gain access to the ultimate target. And they have to do so somehow without being noticed. If an engineer were to expose themselves to multiple people within the organization or group, the changes of being compromised would increase notably. Nobody thinks the same way, so the engineer would have to use different personas against different individuals within the group. Also, it would be extremely time-consuming to create a complete profile of multiple individuals. Even if the engineer spent the time, and did all of this correctly, the risk of the mission going south sand ending badly increases in

ratio with the number of moving elements in a
social engineering job.

The Information Collected So Far

To start narrowing down the list of potential targets, the engineer has to pool all the information collected over the past weeks and rate the targets they have found. Even though certain personality types are perceived to be easier to manipulate and get one's way with, a social engineer always has individual preferences when it comes to choosing targets. So there really is no go-to "template" for this. But let's say our hypothetical social engineer specializes in passive-aggressive individuals.

To create a light profile of that kind of person, the social engineer has to find signs of passive-aggressiveness in his information gathering of individuals up to this point. Signs like: a cynical and aggressive demeanor, continual complaints, not being liked within the group (or company or organization), and more. If the information collected on a given individual matches at least one of these signs, the engineer can start to categorize the potential targets based on personality type and end up with a list that ranks the individuals from "best" to "worst."

Use the Organization's Hierarchy to Decide

With that list as a starting point, the engineer now has to decide on the access levels of each and every one of the potential targets. As I mentioned, every social engineer has an ideal target, and in this case, the social engineer's preferred personality is passive-aggressive. Now the engineer has to make sure that the target has access to—or at the very minimum, valuable information about—the objective. At this point the hierarchy within the group is critical. A leader will, of course, have full access to everything the business does (unless the chairman of the board is really paranoid). The next step in the information gathering process is to assess whether any of the targets have the kind of access needed. If the engineer finds potential targets on the list that do not match their own individual preferences (non-passive-aggressive personality) and who is considered to be at the bottom of the food chain, these individuals can be removed from the list—no need to spend further time and effort on collecting information on them anymore.

As I said, there is no red line here, so it really depends on the engineer how this phase is conducted. To continue the pursuit of the perfect target, the updated list preferably has two to four targets who match one or more of the personality signs and have access to the primary objective in various degrees.

The Weakest of the Weak Links

This list now must be shortened a little more. The engineer will never wholly discard the potential targets at the bottom of the list, but the best strategy would be to split them up into an A- and a B-list. While the A-list consists of preferably one target (two at the most), the B-list is made up of the rest. Consider the B-list as sort of backup targets.

But before the engineer can split the list up, he or she needs to look at a little more of the information gathered so far.

What they are mainly checking for now is that all the relevant information about the target fits their personality preference and that the list is adjusted according to access level, personality, and the last piece of the puzzle: hunger for power. The engineer can easily come to a conclusion about this quality after assessing personality, because it really is, after all, a personality question. That being said, I wouldn't go so far as to claim that these two personality traits (passive-aggressive and power hungry) have a scientific link to each other, so it's better to keep them separate. It really makes a huge difference in any social engineer's mission if the target is craving power and status. An individual who craves attention, power, status, and money will often do almost anything to get it, including shady practices and going out on a limb for a potential profit, and this attitude opens a lot of doors for a social engineer to plan an attack. They might easily make use of a target with this kind of ambition. An individual who does not crave anything other than a safe job and a steady paycheck, on the other hand, won't necessarily risk doing anything shady or go out on that limb for the potential benefit of climbing the ladder of success.

So the list now should be split into two. The A-list should only consist of the individual(s) that the engineer would regard as the weakest link. The weakest link can be summed up as one of these: highest authority, highest security clearance, passive-aggressive, or power hungry (or another label drawn from the store of relevant information gathered already).

Chapter 6.
Recon

With all the information the engineer now possesses, why would he need more? Well, you can take all the technology in the world and use it to find every piece of information that you want, but there remains this truth: Humans will display random behavior. Straight-up technical and physical information gathering will only take you so far. Once you gather information online, you can do a light profile on the target(s), but that's just step one. Step two is confirming the information with real evidence. Real evidence of an individual's behavior can only be gathered by old-school stakeouts and following the target around for a week or two. Web information can be put up on purpose to throw the social engineer off; data can be changed in certain ways to appear different than it really is and to manipulate the system. If a big company hires a social engineer to retrieve confidential information from their own company, it would be considered a social engineering test. It could be done as a security health check (without the employees having been drilled in social engineering already), or it could be a company that puts serious effort into their employees, to make sure they stay safe and are able to prevent and mitigate potential malicious social engineers. If the latter is the case, technical information gathering on its own could be worthless without the confirmation provided by empirical observations.

Individual Observation

Individual observation requires real hands-on work from the engineer. The engineer has to be where the target is, when they are, every day of the week, in order to get the necessary practical information.

This could involve spending some pretty long hours in the car, waiting to see what the target does every day. Having eyes on the individual would mean following them to work, home, to hobbies, exercise, events, dinners, coffee dates, and everything they do in a regular week. The ultimate goal is to nail down their daily and weekly schedule and to ensure that the information retrieved from the technical and physical data gathering matches up with the real day-to-day life of the target.

How does the target live his life? Does his personality match the personality the engineer concluded he would have, or does the target display different personalities with different people? Is the target paranoid in any way? If the target displays noticeably different personalities to different people, it may bring up a red flag for the engineer. If the target behaves like he or she is extremely paranoid, that's also a red flag. Why are these red flags? Because a person like this, who can quickly switch between multiple personalities (we're not talking about being kind to some people and mean to others here, that would just be normal behavior) in a way that shows that they are always in control and have a clear agenda in social situations, usually possesses high social intelligence and reflective capacity. That means that a social engineer, who also has both of these characteristics (usually), will have to go to war, in a sense. I call it a "war" because, with a "normal" individual, the social engineer usually has the upper hand and stays in total control of the situation from start to finish. But in this case, the engineer is meeting a like-minded individual, so to speak. This can turn the table, because the social engineer, instead of working a plan that is well thought through and actionable, now faces the genuine possibility of himself becoming a target (or becoming entangled in a psychological game with the target, which is not preferable, needless to say).

If the target displays paranoid behavior like double-checking locks, taking different routes to work every other day, not following any confirmable routines, staying up oddly late, keeping the curtains closed at home all day, using multiple phones, never going to the same place for groceries twice, and so on, the engineer will know they are in for a tough go of it. Dealing with an individual who checks their rearview mirror for potential tails while driving, "feels" it if someone has been in their home, gets alerted by the smallest of sounds outside, and is acutely aware of their surroundings in general, is not a great situation for a social engineer.

For a social engineer, the job must be abandoned and canceled the moment there arises the slightest of suspicion against the engineer or the situation as a whole. An engineer who proceeds with a target who has doubts about the situation or directly about the engineer will have a rough time getting the job done. Remember, a social engineer's primary objective is to attain the end goal without anybody reacting the slightest bit to what actually happened. It should be perceived as another day at work and business as usual for the target(s), nothing else.

Family

Once the engineer has confirmed the personality characteristics of the target, it's time to get an overview of the important people in his daily life. The things the engineer discovers in this phase go a long way to strengthen the target profile further (or point out details which had perhaps escaped notice before). Does the individual have a spouse and kids or are they single? Are they well off or struggling to pay the bills (tactic: check the mailbox)? What are the professions of the family members who would be considered closest to the individual (tactic: simple social media and Google search)? In the big picture, these are small, not so essential facts about the target, but the knowledge that the target is struggling to pay the bills, for example, could prove to be quite useful in deciding on an attack strategy. Perhaps the target is a complete novice when it comes to computers and technology, so their nephew comes over occasionally to help with tech-related household tasks. And perhaps that nephew is a digital forensic investigator, an ethical hacker, or a security consultant at a large IT firm. The engineer's thirty minutes

spent digging up the professions of the closest
relatives could potentially be thirty well spent
minutes when it comes to planning out an
attack.

Activities, Hobbies, and Interests

While the engineer is observing the target, it's important to think deeper than just comings and goings. What exactly does the target participate in on their spare time? Does it involve sports, support clubs, recreations like golf or bowling, or other hobbies? The information gathered during this stage could potentially create an easy way in for the engineer.

Let's say the target loves golfing, but the engineer doesn't know how to golf, nor could he possibly become proficient within the timeframe of the job. But the engineer can at least take up the sport; they can show up on the golf course every time the target does and practice their skills. After the engineer makes sure that the target has spotted him a couple of times and thereby creates a sense of trust that the engineer isn't just some random person displaying suspicious behavior, they can walk up to the target and give a compliment on the latter's golfing skills. The engineer can say something like: "I'm just starting out, and I'm not really getting the hang of it… Since you're clearly sort of a top player at this golf course, I was just wondering if you had some tips to help me get started."

Just put yourself in the target's shoes for a second. You have a hobby that you're really good at, and you visit the same place frequently for the purpose of this activity. One day, and then over the next several weeks, you notice an individual who keeps showing up and appears to be struggling with the very same thing you have mastered. One day, this slightly frustrated but very humble person comes up to you, praises you, and then asks for some tips on how to improve their skills. Would you do it? Most people will naturally say yes to the request, thereby inviting the engineer into their mind, and then the game is on. (But not the game that the target thinks they are playing.)

The main reason this strategy works so well is because of the common human feeling of wanting to help. Another feeling is at play as well: When the engineer fails again and again and humbly asks for help while paying compliments, it gives the target a sense of superiority over the other—"Of course, I'll help the weaker man." This feeling of authority not only gives the target a boost in confidence, but it also builds a superficial layer of trust with

the engineer. The target will not be likely to
suspect this humble person who can't even golf
to be a dangerous individual who is after
something valuable of his.

Friends

Does the target have close friends that they hang out with regularly? People they trust in a "Hey, I have something I want to tell you, but this is information has to stay between us" kind of way? Do they have close friends but do not frequently hang out with them? Or do they have no friends at all? This information can be useful in many ways in strengthening the profile of the target: By looking at the friends, the engineer can spot irregularities in the target's profile. There is a lot to the saying, "You are who you surround yourself with." If the target surrounds himself with people who display behavior much different than the engineer's profile of the target indicates as characteristic, it might be a good time to head back and take another look at the information gathered so far.

Hangouts

Another piece of information that could prove to be quite valuable to the engineer is the target's favorite hangouts. Whether these are restaurants, bars, or theaters doesn't really matter; what matters is being aware of it, so that the engineer may manipulate it as a way in or as a stepping point to an attack. If the target spends a lot of his time in bars, it can generally be safely inferred that he likes to have a drink or two while he is inside. And if that's the case, it presents an excellent avenue for the social engineer to get what he wants. As we all know, alcohol and secrets don't complement each other very well.

Chapter 7. Further Observations

Shoulder Surfing

"Shoulder surfing" can mean a lot of things, even within the social engineering niche. But in the end, all the recon approaches under this umbrella boil down to spending time close to the target (without the target knowing or thinking twice about it). We're not talking about sitting in a car and watching the target from a distance right now. It's all about the details. The engineer's goal now is to look over the shoulder of the target—be a fly on the wall for a few days, so to speak. If the target goes out for drinks, the engineer goes out for drinks. If the target goes out for dinner, the engineer does the same. What sets this phase apart from the previous recon tactics is that it requires the engineer not only to get close, but to pick the very nearest table at the restaurant, the closest stool at the bar. And this needs to be done in a way that allows the engineer to collect information without raising suspicions. If the engineer is good at what he does, shoulder surfing can result in credit card details, internet browsing habits, confidential information from dinner conversations, and endless other specifics.
The key, as always, is to pay close attention, mine the details, and stay invisible.

Political Standpoint

People who have a clear and decided political standpoint tend to gather frequently in groups and at events with like-minded people. Adopting the same strong and clear political view could serve as an entry for a social engineer. Think about it: When we have strong convictions on a particular issue (especially if we are convicted on issues that make us an underdog, and especially if the issue and its supporters gets harassed in the media), we form a solid bond with other like-minded people. It doesn't matter if they are strangers in every other sense of the word; it's just the way this human phenomenon seems to work. So if an engineer has a target who loves to talk and think politics, they will take note of that, find out the causes which the target cares strongly about, emulate the latter's standpoint, and in the end establish a personal relationship with the target. When the opportunity arises to use emotions to gain the trust and confidence of a target, that's usually a great route to go.

Lies or Secret Life (Leverage)

How many times have you read and watched movies about people living double lives? Taking care of a spouse, kids, and steady job from morning to evening, and going out on criminal enterprises at night? In the most extreme cases, a target might have a kind of "Batman" lifestyle, but that's not what an engineer expects to find out; what's not uncommon is a secret life in the form of a lover, some dealing on the side, work for a competitor, or other questionable behavior. Now, why do these little secrets this even matter? Well, there is a little thing called leverage, and it's a powerful thing to have on your side. It can quickly turn the tables in any kind of social engineering job. If an engineer finds out that the target is engaging in clandestine activities which their boss or family doesn't know about and which would somehow expose or weaken the target if it were to be revealed, the engineer has leverage on the target. They don't necessarily use it for any specific purpose, but they could figure out a way to ethically utilize the information in order to get what is desired from the target. These are rocky grounds to walk on, because the moment an engineer takes a wrong step with the information he's gathered, he has exposed himself to the target (and anybody else involved). We're talking about extortion, blackmail, and threats. (If somebody is engaged in these types of behavior and calls themselves a social engineer, they need a reality check. Because finding that kind of information and leveraging it in the ways I explained above, just makes you a common criminal. Anybody can do that.)

As I've said many times in this book, a professional social engineer's job is not to harm a target in any way. It is to retrieve the information which they were hired to retrieve and in the end to report back to their employer about potential security risks regarding their employees and their facilities.

Chapter 8.
Keep Your Information Safe (How Not To Get Targeted)

In a digital world like this one, it is close to
impossible to keep all your information safe
without going completely off the grid. With
that said, there are a lot of things you can to
do to minimize the risk of becoming a target of
a social engineering attack.

Your Information

All the information you put out on the web ceases to be your own property as soon as you hit that publish button. Sure, we can talk about copyright and privacy laws, but those doesn't change the fact that the information you posted on a social media platform or other website is now accessible to *anyone*, and will be for a long time, no matter what you try to do about it. Hindsight is a good thing, but when it comes to information floating around the worldwide web, think twice before you do something that can endanger you in the future.

You might be thinking, "Oh, but I just posted about my vacation and photos of my newborn kid..." That information would have been complicated for any social engineer to come by without you publishing it yourself. But since you did so, the engineer now knows that you're on vacation in Spain with your three kids and wife. That's information that the engineer did not have before you posted it. And as you've read earlier in this book, these are all elements that go into planning an attack.

Routines and Habits

There's nothing wrong with having a so-called "9-5 lifestyle." You go to work, come home, watch TV, go to sleep, and then do it all over again. Whatever floats your boat, my friend. But, when you do these things day in, day out, week after week and year after year, you start developing some routines. Routines are great for paying your bills on time and making sure your house doesn't resemble deserted festival grounds every third day. But when it comes to your schedule and habits, you should always try to throw in some variation. Doing the same thing every day, at the exact same time, makes you predictable, and being predictable makes you a prime target for any social engineering attack. Mix it up some days: Take the bus instead of your car to work, stop by somewhere on the way home so that you arrive home at 6:30 instead of 5:30. I think you get my point. Not only will this give the engineer a whole different perception of you, but it will also make you yourself more aware of your surroundings. Living a predictable life based on routines and habits tends, in the end, to make any individual sleepwalk through life, thereby unaware of their surroundings and unable to spot potential threats.

Lies and Secrets

Sometimes it's necessary to lie, and sometimes it's necessary to keep a secret from somebody. But always remember that whenever you lie about something, the person you lie to has leverage on you (even if they don't know it). You'll know it, and you'll spend time and energy thinking about that lie—if not consciously, then subconsciously, every day. We're not talking about lying to a friend about some outfit you said was amazing when you really thought it was horrible. We're talking about real lies and deceit. Keep your lies to a minimum and remember: If you have a secret and you tell more than one person about it, it's really not a secret anymore. You have to stay in control of your personal life and relationships in order to be in the safe zone. A person who figures out you lied to them can be easily used by a social engineer to get information about you. A person who once trusted you with a secret, which you then spread around, thereby breaking their trust, can also be turned against you. So, keep your secrets to yourself and your lies to a minimum, be kind to the people who deserve your kindness, and don't spend time and negative energy on others. It will only come back and bite you in the ass later in life.

Reality Check

Some people live in a bubble. They don't read what they don't like to read, they don't educate themselves, and they don't believe that there are real things happening in "shadows" 24/7 in our world today. They live in a cozy place which they've created in their heads, based on only their own friends, family, and experiences in life. If this is you, SNAP OUT OF IT! People who live this way are considered highly valuable targets by a social engineer. They believe what they want to believe; therefore the engineer can manufacture truths about something he knows they're interested in and can create situations they like to be in. He can really make use of his whole arsenal of tools and tactics to get what he wants.

The thing about these naïve people is that they have skepticism for everything outside their comfort zone, but they never actually double-check anything. If the engineer tells them something which supports their existing beliefs in a setting with which they are familiar, they'll usually take the bait immediately. They are the opposite of paranoid, in a way.

This brings me to the next point: Be paranoid. Don't sit in your room and cry all day because you're afraid of the world, but do start double-checking facts, be aware of your surroundings, and keep an eye out for anything that raises your suspicions. I'm not saying you should go crazy with these precautions—that would only ruin your chances of a happy, healthy life. But just get your mind accustomed to the fact that there may be people out there who want to hurt you in one way or another. That's a fact for every human being on this world. There may be people out there who wish to have something we have, and they may try to get it one way or another.

User Accounts

The last advice I have for you regarding information gathering is that you take control over your user accounts. Whenever you register a new account on the web, you deliver your email address, password, and other identifiable information into the hands of another company. You're basically saying: "Here is my data, and I trust you to keep it safe." Sadly, they don't always. With massive data breaches time and time again, even at the biggest IT companies in the world that specialize in your user experience on their platforms, account details get lost. Remember Metasploit? Using that kind of service to get information about you could be really easy for a social engineer if you are careless with details like your email address.

The main tip I have for you regarding this issue is to register a fake email address—an email address you don't use for anything other than your accounts on different services and websites. And make it something random. Don't use a domain you own. You can use Gmail or any other similar provider. Just remember to keep the address unidentifiable. Never use your real name on user accounts if

you don't have to. Create yourself a nickname
that only you know about, and use that
instead. If you want to register a new domain
for your business, pay a little extra to get the
extension that hides your registrar details on
the web. If you do that, and an engineer
searches for information about your domain,
he won't be able to find out anything about
you.

I don't think I have to go into detail on every
single thing you can do to keep your online
information as safe as it can be. What you've
read here covers most of it. To sum it up, don't
be naive, and don't make it easy for anybody to
profile you.

Your Next Steps

First of all, I want to congratulate you! Everyone loves to talk about how they read books, do this, or do that. But very few actually do anything, let alone read a book from start to finish. You have proven that you have the desire and passion to learn the craft that is social engineering and to educate yourself on how to best protect your information. This book has been a massive step in what will turn out to be a fantastic journey for you.

I would love to be your guide on your way to a more in-depth knowledge of social engineering. Therefore I will keep writing books to help you learn everything you need to know.

Remember, the only thing you need to do to get ahead in life is to take action. So keep up the good work, and I hope we cross paths again in the next book in this series.

About the Author

Dennis Lonmo started his first business in 2008. Since then he has been involved in multiple startups and established businesses in different industries. Now, a decade later, he is an author and a highly rated online instructor of students hailing from more than 117 countries worldwide. He runs a consulting business—the very same business that rolled his career into motion all those years ago—as well as a digital and a security agency.

Dennis loves educating and inspiring others to help reach their goals and ambitions in business and in life. Learn more about Dennis at: amazon.com/author/dennislonmo

One Last Thing

Thank you for taking the time to read this book. I really appreciate it.

If you enjoyed it or found it useful, I would be very grateful if you would post a short review on Amazon.com. Your support makes a big difference and I personally read all the reviews so that I can make my next book even better. All you need to do is click the "Review" link on this book's Amazon page.

Thank you for your support!

Dennis Lonmo

Resources

Dradis Framework

https://dradisframework.com/

Maltego CE

https://www.paterva.com/web7/buy/maltego-clients/maltego-ce.php

Whois.net

https://whois.net/

Pipl

https://pipl.com/

Dennis Lonmo

Website

https://dennislonmo.com

Amazon Author Profile

https://amazon.com/author/dennislonmo

Udemy Instructor Profile

https://www.udemy.com/user/dennis-lonmo/